ETHEREAL

Whispers of The Soul

CHACHA ISRAEL

Published by:

ChaCha Israel

Book Cover Design:

Rob Williams

This book is a collection of original poetry and is protected under copyright law. Any resemblance to actual persons, living or deceased, is purely coincidental.

ISBNs:

Paperback: 979-8-9920399-1-7

Hardcover: 979-8-9920399-3-1

First Edition: December 2024

Author Contact Info:

connect@chachaisrael.com

website www.chachaisrael.com

Contents

LIFE'S JOURNEY

LIGHT AND SHADOW

DIVINITY

ETERNAL SOUL MATES, PAST LIVES WHISPER FORBIDDEN, LOVE LOST IN THIS LIFE.

For My Immortal Beloved

Acknowledgments

This journey would not have been possible without the unwavering support of those who have stood beside me through every season of life. To my husband Tim, my mother Lydia, and my children Preston & Kayla, thank you for being my anchor and my light. Your unconditional love and belief in me have been my guiding force. To my mentors and spiritual guides, who have illuminated my path with wisdom and compassion, your teachings have forever shaped my journey.

To the Divine Mother, whose presence I have felt in every sacred ceremony, thank you for guiding me back to myself. And to the souls who have walked with me, whether for a moment or a lifetime, your impact has been indelible.

Lastly, to you, dear reader, thank you for allowing Ethereal to be part of your journey. May these words inspire and ignite the light within you. This book is as much yours as it is mine, a testament to our shared journey.

With gratitude,
Chacha Israel

Love and Longing

Through a Rainbow

As I immerse in the thought of you,
Your gaze finds me...
Piercing the hidden chambers of my heart.
A soft brush of your lips,
A knowing without words,
And for a brief moment,
I surrender to the warmth of your imagined embrace,
A life with you by my side.

The rain patters,
Its gentle rhythm draws me back...
A dream dissolving in the cool, damp air
Of this moment.
Alone in my car,
Moving through the misted rain,
The faint scent of earth rising around me.
I let go, hope slipping away,
Until a rainbow arches from the dark, wet road,
And I pass through it...
Wrapped in light, reminded of our love,

Birthed from the heavens,
A spark that defies the ages.

Divine, immortal, unbreakable...
Though you're not here beside me,
Forever, we shall be.
As rain meets light,
Our love stretches beyond all bounds,
Binding us through the unseen,
Echoing across a world that knows no end.

Distant Yet Bound

Our love, forged in timeless realms,
born from the breath of stars,
two souls spun together,
woven in golden threads of divinity.

But here, in this life,
our paths wind in parallel,
pulled apart by the weight of duties,
by roles we cannot set aside.

Still, my heart feels your presence,
an unspoken bond beneath the surface,
like a quiet current drawing us close,
though life's demands keep us apart.

In moments stolen from routine,
a glance, a touch, a shared silence...
reminders of something deeper,
a pull that no distance can sever.

We move through days as strangers,
yet something in me knows you,
as if in the spaces between,
our souls are still entwined,
waiting for the day we can finally be whole.

Dreamscape

Awakened by the sun,
eyes ablaze,
trapped in the fabric of time,
dream walking through folds of reality.
Memories begin to fade;
sunshine turns to shadow,
an aching yearning in my heart.
Yet the moon rises again,
and now I remember
your embrace.

I close my eyes,
feel you near;
our love pulses
through eternity.

Oh, dreamscape...
my sacred dreamscape...
where I find you,
bound in a celestial embrace

under the lunar gaze.
We are light in the shadows.
I am with you,
my everlasting love...

In this realm, we dance,
where time holds no dominion,
and every heartbeat echoes

the whispers of forever.
In the depths of night,
your essence weaves with mine,
and I am home.

If You Die Today

If you die today
Could you say you loved deeply
Our souls entwined...

Eternal Love

For a moment... just a heartbeat...
time stood still.
I embraced the essence of immortality,
awakened to the truth within,
arriving to greet my soul,
bathed in the radiant light of creation,
where I merged with the cosmos,
a journey through a million stars,
each a whisper of eternity.

Pure bliss enveloped me,
the secrets of existence unveiled,
and in that moment of clarity,
I remembered who I am.
When I gazed into your eyes,
my soul danced with recognition,
a sacred reflection.

And then I knew,
my destination all along was you...

the heartbeat of my existence,
the anchor of my dreams,
the flame that ignites my spirit.
In your embrace, I am whole,
woven into the fabric of love,
where time and space dissolve,
and all that remains is us.

In this eternal moment,
we are the creators of our own infinity,
bound not by time, but by the depth of our connection,
a love that transcends the stars,
illuminating the path ahead,
leading us home.

Shangri-La of You

Life on the fast track,
a glorious solo act,
energy bubbling up,
each moment electrified,
high as the Kunlun Mountains,
elevated, centered, alive.

Then, a song drifts in,
humming me from reality.
Time slows,
and I glide down,
into a valley of memory,
a Shangri-La of you.

I pause and let go,
flowing into all I've missed...
my heart aches for you,
still longing,
missing you,
always.

. . .

Heart's Echo

Hum drum
Hum drum
Hypnotic pulse
drowning the ache
of living
without you
by my side.

Hum drum
Hum drum
I march on
with leaden chains,
shackles weighing heavy,
walking through
the weight of the universe...
Crux I bear,
a karmic debt
I must repay,
the past trailing behind me,
holding me back.

15

Hum drum
Hum drum
oh, my beating heart
echoes
into the abyss
as it fades away,
a slow death
of non-existence.
You're a warmth
lingering beyond reach,
so close
yet so far.

Hum drum
Hum drum
I lay to rest,
hoping for
one last salvation,
yearning for
one last kiss,
one last embrace.

But in this life,
I know
we can never be.

Until one final breath,
unable to voice my final wish...
I fade into stillness.

Lotus Heart

Senses flooded her soul,
a lotus blossoming
from the muddy bed
where life pulses,
where roots reach deep, unseen,
and strength is born in shadow.

Her heart stirred,
a quiet murmur at first,
then a surge, a spark,
as if struck by lightning,
a volt through her veins,
shaking her awake
to a monsoon of love,
pouring down like warm rain,
filling every hollow,
every forgotten space.

Yet sadness gripped her heart,
a gentle ache woven into joy,

like clouds that linger
after the rain has passed.

She felt the pull of longing,
an echo of all she'd known,
the remnants of past sorrows
still tethered to her roots.

With each beat, a strange harmony...
love's pulse dancing with grief,
a fragile bloom carrying both,
like petals folded to hold
both the light and shadow.

In the stillness of her blossoming,
she embraced the flood,
each tear a part of the monsoon,
each ache a note in love's song.

A lotus rising,
rooted in both joy and sorrow,
she bloomed as she wept,
and in that tender duality,
she became whole.

Unrequited

If you could only see
deep within my heart,
buried beneath layers,
veiled in shadowed depths...

If you could only hear
the pulse of my soul,
the deafening silence
each time I call your name...

If you could only taste
tears of never-ending flow,
a raging river of untamed force,
an unrequited longing...

If you could only feel
the heat of my skin,
waves of wanting,
waiting for you to claim...

I am here,
yearning
for you...
reach for me.

Presence

Fronted by solitude,
stripped bare of adornments,
without decadence to drape me,
or a single material thing
to raise me high.

Here, I stand unclothed,
nothing left to barter with,
nothing to shield my skin
from the quiet gaze of truth.

In the hollow of this emptiness,
where walls do not whisper
and silence lays its heavy hand,
I felt the presence of God...
not in the grandiose,
not in the gilded heights,
but in the soft descent of stillness
that settled like a breath.

Unburdened, I lingered,
not seeking elevation,
but grounded, humbled, small...
a single soul before the vastness,
welcoming the whisper
that needed no sound.

Cosmic Love

With cosmic portals wide open,
you and I,
the helix of eternity,
moving as one.

Masculine divine,
feminine divine,
our hearts converge
in love's eternal dance,
echoing through the cosmos,
a symphony of stars.

You and I,
ancients of the ages,
keepers of the light,
birthing a new world
through the will of our love,
boundless and true.

Together we weave

the threads of existence,
infusing each moment
with radiant essence,
transforming shadows
into luminous dawn.

In the embrace of stars,
we create our own universe,
where love knows no bounds,
and the cosmos sings
our song of forever,
echoing through time.

The Only One

There's only One
that I seek,
only One
my heart endlessly yearns for.
Eyes that hold the universe,
touch that caresses the very essence of me,
a voice vibrating through my soul,
each syllable a gentle embrace,
each whisper a sacred promise.

Heart beating in rhythm with mine,
a symphony of two souls entwined.
As I lay down to sleep,
dreams weave us together,
and as dawn awakens,
I search for that same heartbeat...
yearning for the only One
who matters most,
the only One
who infinitely cradles my heart.

In the quiet stillness,
I feel your presence linger,
like the first light of day,
a reminder that love endures,
that in this vast expanse of existence,
you are my anchor,
my guiding star.

In every breath, I find you,
in every heartbeat, you are there,
a constant melody playing softly,
echoing through the corridors of my mind.
So, I surrender to this love,
this exquisite, transcendent bond,
knowing that with you,
I am whole.

For you are the pulse in my veins,
the essence of my dreams,
and as I awaken to the world,
it is your light I seek,
the only One
who holds my heart
in the tender embrace of eternity.

Enkindled

For a moment,
let me stop time,
linger on your kiss...
its ember, reigniting,
a flame from my soul's sleep,
the myth of beauty reborn.

I was the one,
frozen in shadows,
until you reached me,
your touch stirring embers,
awakening warmth
from the quiet of winter.

And you, my rescue, my fire,
rising through every darkened vein,
igniting what had dimmed.

No longer will I run,
I am here, rooted in the blaze,
found in the burn of love's light.

I am here to stay.

Transformation and awakening

Shekinah Awakening

I rise, fierce and eternal,
woven from threads of the cosmos,
my essence steeped in stardust and soil,
grounding my feet as the cosmos pulses.
I am the boundless love of the Great Mother,
the wisdom of ancient goddess light,
the Shekinah's holy presence,
and the deep, untamed roar of earth itself.

For years, I wandered, hollow in the shadows,
my spirit unbound yet homeless, aching for its place,
my truth lost under the weight of others' wants,
hidden, fragments scattered by their demands.
But suffering called me inward,
and there, in fertile darkness,
I found the seeds of my own becoming,
my heart pulsing with the weight of the heavens.

I drank from the breath of the earth,
Ayahuasca's tendrils entwined my heart, warm and fierce,

seeping through veins, rooted in the marrow,
awakening the divine within my depths.
In the Amazon, I met my gaze in jaguar eyes,
my shadow dancing, light and dark as one.
Under the Arabian sky of Wadi Rum, I became the desert itself...
sun warmed, wind carved, and endless,
each breath a prayer:
Remember who you are.

I rise, boundless and whole,
divine feminine and masculine merging as one,
the pulse of the Infinite echoing in my chest.
I stood as creator and protector,
a union of seed and flame,
yin and yang within my soul.

I am here to unfold, to surrender wholly
to the divine blueprint, letting myself flow
where river, wind, earth, and fire go,
to simply exist, imperfect as perfection.

I rise, now walking with the power of storms,
no longer bound by names others bestow,
simply shining light as a testament
to my own transformation.
For I know what it is to hunger for love
in places it cannot be found.
I hear their whispers of longing, their fears echoing,
shame like a pulse beneath the surface,
and beneath it all, the flicker of sacred light,
the Shekinah's gentle call, guiding them back to wholeness.

I rise, once lost in slumber's hold, now a storm,
a voice of truth, a beacon in darkness,
my heart ablaze.
I carry Artemis's wild, moonlit stride,

Durga's strength, like rooted stone, in my bones,
Inanna's ascent, fierce as dawn, from the underworld,
and Hatshepsut...ancient pharaoh who defied the norm,
a testament to the merging of divine masculine and feminine.

I know I am here to embody the beauty of creation,
to be a beacon unto myself, radiant and whole,
a presence of light simply unfolding.

I rise and rise again.... unstoppable, unbound,
a testament to the Infinite,
a torch lighting unknown paths,
a flame that burns beyond sight, into the vast unknown.

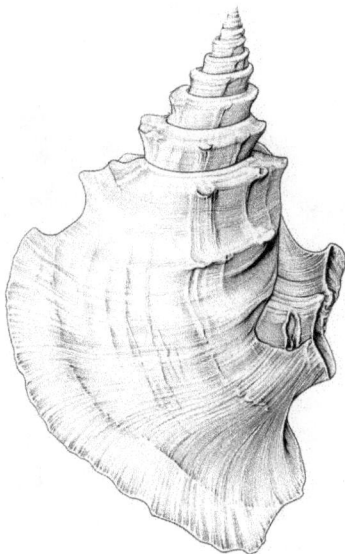

Metamorphosis

When it feels like everything
is slipping through your fingers,
when you sense the ground giving way,
and it's the darkest night of your soul,
where the ache is too sharp to bear,
and you've become the raging wind
of the hurricane itself,
spiraling fast into a vacuum of shadows...

Let go... let go... release that tight grip.
Be that wind.
Embrace the knowing,
flow and move with it.
Heed its call... there's nothing to fear,
nothing to control.
You are passing through
the birth canal of life itself.
Yes... you are being reborn.

This is all part of your soul's journey,

a golden passage set in motion,
a gateway to new beginnings.
Move through the pain,
shed your skin like cracked armor,
let it fall, piece by piece... yes, allow it!
The ache may be fierce,
but it's only a moment.

You are built to withstand so much more...
a Herculean spirit of strength and will.
Endure it... but stay true to yourself.
Stand firm against the voices of others.
Embrace the cost,
for magnificence awaits you.
Let go... and center in acceptance.

It will be as it should.
You've always held the reins,
the creator of your destiny,
living the sacred design within,
crafted beyond this fleeting now,
a step toward all you are becoming.

So step forward,
unfurling your spirit like wings against the storm,
knowing each pain, each scar, is a vow to yourself...
a pledge to rise, whole and unbreakable.
You are the dawn of your own making,
an ember stoked into fire, blazing forward...
a testament to self-love, fierce and undeniable.

Free Falling

letting go,
diving deep,
free falling...
a leap of faith
into love.

naked and unguarded,
soul revealed;
kundalini rising,
I soar on breathless wings,
wide open,
embracing you.

no questions linger,
nothing asked in return;
loving you is enough,
the essence of existence,
the heartbeat of my soul.

in this sacred trust,

I find my freedom...
a dance of hearts,
infinite and true.
for in your love,
I am home,
and here, I truly live.

Into the Heart of Ayahuasca

I stepped into my spirit,
barefoot on the trembling earth,
and surrendered to the currents,
the unknown depths of awakening
that called to me from beyond...
a voice from my own soul, ancient and wise,
whispering, Come home.

In Costa Rica's verdant heart,
I felt the pulse of the earth beneath me,
drank from the cup of Ayahuasca,
and watched my edges blur and fade.
Vines wrapped around my heart,
unearthing buried fears,
and I was stripped, bare as the roots,
left only with truth...
the quiet fire of my soul's longing,
and the first sparks of transformation.

Through the Amazon jungle of Iquitos, Peru,

I wandered deeper, darker, wilder,
where the ceiba trees stood like ancient sentinels,
their roots gripping secrets of the earth.
Under the stars, I drank,
letting the sacred plant medicine take me,
and visions poured like rivers,
carving new paths through the valleys of my mind.
Jaguar eyes met mine,
holding a mirror to my own shadow,
and I learned to dance with it,
to be both light and dark, whole and broken,
as the jungle sang the song of my rebirth.

To the red sands of Wadi Rum, Jordan,
I traveled with the desert winds,
where the caves whispered old stories,
and each grain of sand was a prayer.
Under the vast, unbroken sky,
I took the medicine again,
felt the universe swell within me,
every heartbeat a wave,
every breath a sacred chant,
and I touched the edge of eternity,
a place where all was one...
the stars, the earth, and I.

With every sacred plant,
with every cup, every ceremony,
I shed the skin of what I thought I was,
letting the spirit of each place
reawaken something ancient within me.
In visions and in dreams, I saw...
we are the rivers and roots,
the sand and the stone,
the fire and the rain,
woven into the vast tapestry of all that is.

I flowed with my soul's journey,
from Costa Rica's lush forests
to the heart of the Amazon,
to the silence of Jordan's desert,
and I returned, reborn, re-formed...
no longer bound, but boundless,
a drop in the ocean of spirit,
forever flowing
with the pulse of all creation.

Mountains of Khorasan

In the steps of the Gods, I walk,
blindly traversing the path of the Divine.
Each step vibrates with unwavering faith,
guided solely by the sacred songs of Mother.
I stumble through the majestic mountains
of the Great Khorasan,
an odyssey of epic proportions...
this journey leads me to the heart of Aya.

In Her temple, I enter,
an open-heart trembling with anticipation.
Reaching out, I seek a hand,
with His Icaro breath
and Her holy grail.
I drink the nectar from an ancient chalice;
the wisdom of the Goddess flows
through my veins, igniting my spirit.

Aho! Blindness no more...
with eyes wide open,

43

I finally see;
there you stand,
my destiny illuminated.
I embrace the truth of our connection,
knowing that in this moment,
I am home.

Here, in this sacred embrace,
where time and space dissolve,
I find my essence woven
into the fabric of love,
where every heartbeat sings
the melody of eternity.

Peaks of Wadi

Footsteps on rocky peaks,
a soul's ascension,
magnified in moonlight,
a revelation
gifted but to a few.

Breathing in sands of creation,
a landscape raw, magnificent,
each step unearthing ancient wonders.
I awaken, returning
to the essence of You.

For a moment,
dimensions faded...
memory flooding, tears flowing,
nourishing a scorched heart
on holy grounds.

Divine love rises,
unshackled, defying

laws forged by men.
in remembrance, we emerge,
unveiled as timeless beings,
echoes of gods
and stars.

Blessed by Mother,
She who heals,
She who hears,
She who reveals
truth.
this heart beats
across time, through space...
this heart, forever,
Yours.

The Divine Feminine

Inanna's Veil

Goddess divine, cloaked in shadow's grace,
Stood at the altar, in a haunting embrace.
Her wings foregone, yet spirit aglow,
In the stillness of night, where dark rivers flow.

Whispers of power drift in the midnight air,
Echoes of secrets and dreams laid bare.
She weaves the threads of fate's silent loom,
Crafting beauty from chaos, emerging from gloom.

Darkness of creation, a fertile womb,
Where stars are born and shadows consume.
Her gaze, a tempest, fierce and profound,
In the depths of her eyes, the lost can be found.

She dances with shadows, a ballet of night,
Illuminating truths that slip from our sight.
Her laughter, a spell that enchants the air,
Calling forth the lost, the forgotten, the rare.

In the realm of the unseen, she finds her might,
A flower that blooms in the darkest of night.
For in her embrace, the world comes alive,
In the heart of the night, we learn how to thrive.

So here at the altar, where darkness ignites,
We honor the goddess who brings forth the light.
For she is the keeper of stories untold,
In the dance of the night, her legend unfolds.

As shadows retreat, and dawn draws near,
We breathe in the magic, the power, the fear.
For in this sacred space, her essence we trace,
Inanna's veil, a timeless embrace.

Secrets of the Oiran

Snowcapped mountaintop,
grand land of the rising sun,
muse of the Far East.

Lilac and almond,
light notes flirting with spring wind,
pink cherry blossoms.

Steps of the eight swirl,
okobo graze sacred ground,
lips painted sakura.

Artisan of love,
kimono of finest silk,
a fluttering smile.

Divine feminine,
a carnival of hidden masks,
songstress of longing.

Revered by nobles,
ensnared by the empire's gaze...
beloved muse of East.

Beneath white powder,
an Oiran's silent heart,
bound, waiting to breathe.

Last Aria

Do you feel me, love?
The depth of my soul's desire...
see with my heart's eyes?

Bound by destiny,
so close, like shadowed breath, yet
forever out of reach.

Here I slowly fade,
sinking into endless dark...
my love silenced whole.

Like the dying swan,
my final song calls to you...
feel and hear my plea.

Pearl of the Orient

Pearl of the Orient,
Daughter of dawn's first embrace,
Crowned in sacred light.

Eden of the East,
Gaia's unspoiled gift of green,
Beauty's resting place.

Sapphire waves arise,
As whales sing songs to the sky...
Thalassophile's dream.

Smiles like morning sun,
Warm, pure as island breezes...
Ode to innocence.

Sweet chocolate hills rise,
Cradle of eternal peace,
Image of the gods.

Heart beats with your pulse,
Dear beloved Philippines,
Forever my muse.

La Luna

Abracadabra...
throbbing, beckoning,
La Luna stirs
from her tranquil slumber.
She rises in full glory,
dancing, weaving
her ethereal beauty
across the dark expanse...
radiant, ever bright,
illuminating
the hearts of wandering souls.

Surging, urging,
a tidal wave of desire,
a craving that pulls
only for you.
The serpent coils,
magnetic, hypnotic,
majestic, as the full moon
watches over me.

Thoughts of you,
whispers of your name
flow from my heart.

Abracadabra...
I linger here,
yearning for you
to return
to the warmth of my embrace,
to the haven of my arms.

Beloved Mother

One who's undefined,
unbound by the laws of men,
blazing her own path.

Epic heroine,
where no Titan stands a chance,
she wields sacred strength.

Battles fought and won,
victories carved from sheer will,
scars worn as armor.

We stand here defined,
proud witnesses of your light,
beacons through dark nights.

We honor you here,
cherishing each breath we take...
your pain healed through love.

From spirit's deep well,
unapologetic queen,
we love you, Mother.

Lily of The Nile

In the stillness of now,
I cradle a chalice brimming
with the essence of the blue lotus,
the lily of the Nile.

As I sip, I am drawn
into its ancient embrace,
its petals whispering secrets
of a time long past.

The spirit of the Nile
courses through me,
a sacred flow that bridges worlds.

Each sip is a communion,
a dance of my soul
with this celestial bloom.

I am lifted,
floating on the fragrance of divinity,

feeling the gentle caress
of its blue petals against my being.

In this moment,
I am both earth and sky,
human and divine,
forever intertwined
with the ethereal grace
of Egypt's sacred flower.

Rapunzel's Reverie

I sit,
trapped in Rapunzel's tower,
but the doors are wide open,
and light spills across the floor,
inviting me to step beyond,
to cross the threshold
where life waits, trembling,
filled with the warmth of your gaze,
the quiet strength of your hands.

Yet here I linger,
wrapped in shadows,
held by an invisible tether...
a thread of fear, or doubt,
woven from years of solitude,
of dreams kept hidden,
and whispers stilled.

Oh, my beloved,
if only you knew how my soul aches,

how it strains against the silence,
longing to be freed,
to walk into the world with you
as if we'd been born for this.

I imagine your face in every soft reflection,
the way your laughter would echo,
filling these barren walls with light,
and in my heart, I am already running to you,
my feet brushing the earth,
bare and unburdened,
drawn to the gravity of your love.

Why do I hesitate,
held back by fears like silken chains?
I reach for the life I crave,
but my hands fall empty,
clutching the air,
the shadows of what could be,
while the open door beckons,
promising your warmth,
a place beside you that waits unclaimed.

My beloved,
I am tired of longing alone,
tired of dreams caught in an endless loop,
turning in this hollow tower.

One day soon,
I will rise, step across the light,
and leave this haunted place behind.
I will meet you where the world begins,
where the sky opens like a vast promise,
and I will feel the earth beneath us
as we stand together, whole.

Until then, I sit in silence,
my heart a restless storm,
holding its breath, waiting
for the courage to walk through,
to embrace the life
that waits in your arms.

Under the Moonlight

Under the moonlight's silvery gaze,
at the cradle of life,
the river rushes like a heartbeat,
cicadas flamenco, their rhythms wild,
while the wolf's howl echoes through the stillness,
silenced in reverence to the moment.
Center staged upon Gaia's sacred ground,
she stands, a beacon of light and grace,
hand over heart,
feeling the pulse of the earth
beneath her bare feet.

In that sacred stillness,
the glow of the divine envelops her,
the sanctity of sight igniting delight,
for the hour was nigh,
'twas the songbird's last aria,
a symphony woven in twilight threads.

A song of magic fills the air,

a sigil etched in fate's fabric,
an ode to the holy grail of existence,
she lifts her chalice,
drinking deep from Odin's cup,
an offering of grace
that flows through her veins,
a sacrifice of being made whole.

With every note, she sings her truth,
an invocation to awaken the slumbering hearts,
her olive branch extends,
the whisper of love carried on the wind...
'tis the songbird's dying song,
her aria of love,
to awaken those lost in shadows,
reminding them of their light.

In this sacred communion,
the heavens listen,
and the stars shimmer in approval,
for her melody dances across the cosmos,
stirring souls with the essence of longing,
the promise of rebirth cradled in harmony.

Oh yes,
this is for you and me,
a timeless echo in the night,
a reminder that love's song
can transcend the silence,
drawing us back to the sacred,
to the magic woven through existence,
to the heartbeat of the universe,
where all is connected,
and every ending
is but a prelude to another beginning.

Unrequited Love of A Goddess

Spiders weave her threads,
beware of Hecate's brew...
her heart waits, unseen.

Maiden, Crone, and Queen,
in shadows her web is spun;
drink not from her cup.

A hero's pulse seized,
golden chalice, venom sweet...
her love left to burn.

Oh, captive Magi,
bound in Jinn's dark enchantment,
break free of her spell.

Life's Journey

Pathways of The Heart

Even the bravest souls tremble,
shaken by the presence of their Beloved,
vulnerability wrapped in fragrance,
leaving imprints on the heart,
echoes of forgotten dreams.

I remember you, a cryptic carving,
etched in Khemet's ancient scrolls,
where reverence mingles with meaning,
each scent whispering tales divine.

I dance like a wild stream,
flowing between the palms of God,
unshackled movement,
my love for you, a timeless current...
mirroring galaxies, intoxicated
by the brilliance of reflection.

You are silence amid clamor,

an island in the sea of noise;
your quietude speaks volumes,
a voice woven from starlight's fabric.

Tonight, I am Rumi,
the poet of poets,
calling to you, oh Beloved,
Sun of the Suns!
Your face dissolves in moonlight,
where shadows intertwine with dreams;
I wander through night's corridors,
seeking you amidst whispers.

Light becomes a veil,
shrouding your sacredness;
moonlight envelops you,
a pearl in my heart's depths,
its luster a testament to your grace.
You move with the tides,
ever departing, yet leaving
the fragrance of devotion.

At the crossroads we meet,
where breath transforms to life,
and like a breath...immersed, formless,
we scatter, finding essence
in love's alchemy,
where life is a passage,
a doorway to our secret garden.

In this sacred space,
the universe whispers
the secrets of our entwined souls,
timeless, boundless,
each heartbeat a promise,

each sigh a celebration
of love that endures,
forever blooming in eternity.

Beyond the Mirror

Face the whispers of your soul,
step down from the rush of haste,
its speed pulling you from truth,
away from the noise of the world,
echoes of others' expectations.

Unclench your fists,
veins taut, ready to burst.
Loosen your jaw, heavy with restraint,
and release the breath you've held so tightly.

Feel... just feel.

Steer clear... refuse the icy shield
freezing your heart.

Don't be afraid.
Surrender to raw reality,
feel the pull of the sea,
an ancient force as deep as the soul,

calling you back to the vastness within.

The sea beckons,
its waves rocking you to remembrance...
the ocean, clear as glass, a mirror
reflecting who you've become.
Who's looking back?
Does the reflection hide or reveal?
Can you see the self you've long hidden away?

Step off the shaky raft of hollow beliefs,
and dive deep into the ocean's embrace,
where silence and depth reveal life's true essence...
not the material but the ethereal.
Here, in stillness, the soul awakens,
rising like the tide to meet you,
no longer a whisper but a call,
inviting you to a conversation with yourself,
to live beyond numb surfaces.

Stand wide eyed before the wave of fear,
let it crash upon you and strip away false walls,
for its fear's force that frees you,
washing away phantoms,
leaving only the vastness of truth.

Descend through forgotten ache,
to the depths where your higher self waits
in quiet stillness.
Break the surface in an ocean of tears.
Catch your breath... then let go.

Do you recognize this self?
A soul shaped by life,
caught in fleeting glimmers,
bound by unseen chains...

chains forged in duty to others,
woven tight,
suffocating the quiet call of your heart.

Is there a shadow of dreams you once chased,
a hint of forgotten desires?
Does a spark of who you were linger in your eyes?
What truth lies beneath the surface?

Pain is a passage...

a way to know you're alive,
to see the beauty within.

Soften... and breathe.
Feel warmth pulsing within the wound,
for it's the cure to melt
the frosty shell you've formed.

Only then,
by immersing yourself in feeling,
will you step through freedom's gates
and into happiness.

Surrender and let go.
Let life's current carry you,
leading you to your soul's embrace,
to love's essence, deep as the ocean floor.

For, beloved, you've always known...
you are the architect of illusion.

Release your hold.

Step down from the rush of haste,
surrender, my love...

and finally, be free,
like waves dissolving
into the open sea,
merging with the vast, quiet peace deep within,
where, in the quiet portal of your soul's depth,
I stand waiting for you,
and in union, we become whole,
as divinity intended.

Fragments of One

I have journeyed this world
and beyond,
stepping through layers
of unseen dimensions,
seeking truth, chasing light,
yearning for the awakening
of my soul.

Parallel worlds swirl around me
past, present, future...
I gather fragments of my spirit,
piece by luminous piece,
like stars cast into the vast unknown,
each one a spark of lives lived,
a mosaic masterpiece unfolding.

I trace the threads of countless paths,
woven from shadows and light,
connecting a thousand journeys,
an endless tapestry of moments,

each step pulling me closer
to the shape of my own becoming.

Only to find at the heart of it all,
the whole is an image of you...
Yes,
in this reflection,
I know now:
you've been here all along.

Crossroads

There are crossroads
where you stand,
face to face with truth...
the choice pressing,
a path beckoning toward change.

For staying still,
at some point,
is no longer an option.
a step must be taken,
and your soul must embrace
the unknown.

For to walk this path
is to meet courage,
to dive into a new dimension,
armed only with faith
glowing steady in your chest.

This is what it means
to live unbound,
to see with the heart,
to move forward
with the blinders off.

Lessons

After a while, you learn
the quiet difference
between holding a hand
and chaining a soul.
that love doesn't mean leaning
and company isn't security.

You learn
you can't always be what they want,
and how new, shining things
distract and fade.

You begin to see
that kisses aren't contracts,
and gifts aren't promises.
you accept your losses,
head up, eyes forward...
with the grace of a warrior,
not the grief of a child.

You learn
to build your roads on today,
for tomorrow's ground is too uncertain.
those who wish to build
lay their roots deep,
yet even futures fall
mid-flight.

After a while, you learn
even sunshine burns
if you take too much.
pure light, too, can blind.

So you plant your own garden,
decorate your own soul,
instead of waiting
for someone to bring you flowers
or recognize your worth.

And you learn
you truly can endure,
you are stronger than you knew,
your worth isn't negotiable.

You love well,
and you learn
and you learn.
with every goodbye, you learn.

Spring's Embrace

Lovely fern unfurls,
majestic waltz with the breeze,
emerald splendor.

Awake to spring's light,
tender tendrils softly stretch,
basking in warm sun.

Eternal Threads

A love birthed from billions,
and eons of time eternal,
two souls woven from
the golden threads of divinity,
spun in realms where stars first sparked.

We drifted through the heavens,
danced on the edge of the cosmos,
bound by a promise
that outlasted galaxies,
an ancient vow carved in the fabric of light.

Yet here, in earthly form,
our memories lie veiled,
lost beneath the heaviness of mortal form,
and all we know is an ache,
a pull we cannot name,
an echo of something once whole.

In the quiet moments,

when shadows stretch long and time slips,
our souls remember...
a touch, a glance, fragments of a song
whispered in another realm,
as if hidden in the spaces
between each heartbeat.

But in this mortal dance,
our minds wander,
fading beneath earthly burdens,
caught in the web of what we must forget
to learn anew.

Still, I see you...
a flicker beneath the familiar gaze,
a warmth that stirs in depths unnamed,
and though words cannot shape it,
my soul knows yours,
guided by invisible threads,
an undeniable pull.

And so I wait,
until memories rise like mist,
until the veil lifts and light returns,
for in the depths of this incarnation,
we live as strangers...
yet somewhere beyond, we remember:
we are whole.

Light and Shadow

The Edge of Madness

Love is no whisper,
it's wildfire,
an ember in the dark
that blazes fierce,
uncontrolled, wild,
unashamed.
It's the fever
you'd gladly burn for,
a madness
only lovers understand.

Fall, fall recklessly,
headlong, abandon all sense,
leap into the abyss,
heart first,
without guardrails or plans.
Find the one
whose soul strikes yours
like flint on stone,
igniting the spark

that lights your deepest dark.

And how do you find them?
Forget logic, forget fear,
cast away that armor of reason,
and listen...
listen to your heart's raw ache,
its stubborn whisper:
more, more, more.

Because to make the journey
and never fall hard,
to walk the edge
but never jump...
is to wander through life asleep,
missing the sweet, fierce ache
of being utterly, wildly alive.

So risk it all, risk yourself,
because to love like this,
to love like madness,
to try even once...
is to finally know
what it is to live.

Crumbs for a Queen

Was it worth the crown,
that gilded weight, the throne's cold gleam?
A kingdom claimed, love cast away...
now lifetimes later, here I stand,
reborn, with longing still in hand.

In ages past, I ruled and reigned,
traded my heart for power's gain,
lost the fire that would not fade...
a soul's true light, a lover's name.

Now, here in flesh once more,
I pay my penance, silent, sore...
an empty chair beside my throne,
echoes of a love long gone.

Once, I held stars,
whole galaxies within my grasp,
and for that fierce, forbidden spark,
I bartered all...his hand, his heart.

What good is rule if love lies still?
What wealth can quell this endless ache,
to feel his warmth, to trace his face,
yet know he walks another's path,
while I...a stranger to his past.

A thousand lives, I wait, I burn,
in shadows watch his soul return...
each glance a crumb, each word a spark,
to feed the hunger in the dark.

Oh, cruel rebirth, to teach anew
the cost of crowns, the price of rule;
for queens may rise, and empires fall,
but without love, what is it all?

I sit in silence, fate laid bare...
true love, once lost, is seldom spared.

The Witch's Guise

Oh cunning witch,
three-eyed, green-cast crone,
heed not her whispered spells...
a veil of words and incense,
thirsting for gold, myrrh,
the Magi's soul.

Imposter she is
of the Divine Mother,
her guise of woven gold
lures a king to counsel false,
and severs his heart
from love's true flame.

Oh, clever trickster,
draped in glistening lies,
renounce her! Cast her out!
She drains the light of soul's spark,
cursing a king to wither
alone in shadows deep.

. . .

Ashes of Defiance

Lightning strikes through me,
sparking embers from the dark,
flame rekindled whole.

Atriums now steel,
battle forged ventricles quake,
walls once soft, now strong.

Lava flows within,
seismic pulses through hollow
veins in fierce rhythm.

Dormant no longer,
this volcanic heart erupts,
fury blazing free.

If I must become
Phoenix from ashen remains,
I breathe fire anew.

This heart rages on,
thousand forbidden desires,
tempest unyielding.

Defying the gods,
I burn, I rise, to love you...
beyond fate's design.

Blink

Sands of time flow, soft yet sure,
a river of moments, fine and pure,
slipping through fingers like golden lace,
a fleeting dance we dare not chase.

The hours fall, each grain a spark,
brief glimmers cast within the dark...
a hypnotic pull, this slow descent,
lulling hearts in soft lament.

Beware the draw of illusion's sway,
lest life's bright dreams just drift away.
This quicksand tide will steal your breath,
each heartbeat sinking toward the depths.

Seize this pulse, this fragile thread,
before the final grain is shed.
Within a blink of an eye, life ceases...
awake, arise, to life's embraces.

Feel each beat, each wild grace,
for when the last grain slips to dust,
and time holds nothing more in trust,
only moments lived full and true
are those that forever remain with you.

A Breath at a Time

A breath at a time,
there is really only now,
and yet I slip back.

Softly, quietly,
those sweet memories return...
times I had with you.

Just for a moment,
I allow myself to drift,
held by the echoes.

In the stillness here,
I sit with these emotions,
a tender longing.

Each sigh, a whisper;
each heartbeat, a fragile pull
to moments we knew.

The present fades thin,
and I feel the shadows grow,
each one shaped like you.

But with closed eyes still,
you are beside me once more,
a memory's grace.

A breath at a time,
I let go, and you linger,
held close between breaths.

Amrita's Loss

From this cup,
I poured,
love given freely,
abundantly,
from mine to yours,
Amrita flowing
through the currents of time.

I endured,
holding fast as the chalice brimming with light,
but now, my gold has sifted to dust.

How is it so?
I can no longer pour,
I can no longer fill.
And now I see,
my cup is empty...
it was never touched by yours.

And now, empty as silence, I drift...

Divinity

Twas the Night of the Ninth Blue Moon

'Twas the night of the ninth blue moon,
when shadows danced in silver light,
the great wolf howls his ancient song,
a haunting melody piercing the stillness.
Blue Kachina twirls beneath the starlit sky,
swaying to the rhythm of midnight,
as echoes call forth the unseen,
whispers of destiny linger on the breeze.

Just as final judgment looms,
the wheel of fate begins to turn,
the threads of prophecy entwine,
weaving tales of love and longing.
Divine love awakens from its slumber,
stirring the hearts of those who dare to dream.
All bear witness to the miracle of creation,
a sublime convergence in sacred space,
where the cosmos holds its breath.

In this celestial ballet,

the moon and the Great Wolf meet,
a union of souls divine,
intertwining in a dance as old as time.
'Tis now that prophecy unfolds,
as the veil between worlds grows thin,
revealing the secrets of the universe,
the wisdom of ages past,
calling forth the brave and the true.

Under the gaze of the blue moon's glow,
the air shimmers with promise,
and the earth trembles in anticipation,
for from this union springs new life,
the birth of a world yet unformed,
where love reigns supreme and unyielding,
igniting the hearts of all who wander.

In this moment of awakening,
the stars conspire to light our way,
and the howls of the wolf become an anthem,
echoing through valleys and mountains,
a reminder that we are all connected,
woven into the fabric of existence,
each heartbeat a testament to the power
of love that transcends the mundane.

'Tis now, as the night unfolds its tapestry,
the dawn of a new world begins to rise,
where dreams and reality intertwine,
and the essence of creation flows freely.
Embrace this moment,
hold it close like the warmth of a lover's embrace,
for in the dance of the blue moon,
we find our place, our purpose,
and together, we ignite the fire of our souls.

Odyssey of Love

Love calls you forth,
onward through intricate paths,
twisting like ancient vines...
a hydra of endless roads,
each turn a choice, a chance to rise.

Into the unknown you journey,
where shadows waltz and secrets sigh,
a hall of mirrors reflecting
the dreams and fears entwined within.

Here, you must choose...
pause, let the stillness settle;
to stand still is to yield to oblivion.
Ignite your heart's fierce flame,
embrace the fire that defies the void,
a spirit wild and unafraid of the dark.

With each step, uncertainty beckons,
yet love's radiant light illuminates,

a beacon guiding through the labyrinth,
turning the night into a tapestry of day.

So take a breath,
cast aside the weight of doubt;
let courage flow through your veins...
for love, in its purest form,
is a wild, untamed blaze,
a force that transforms the mundane.

Embrace this odyssey,
the threads of fate unraveling;
within your heart's sacred chambers
lies the power to create and heal.

In love's grand design,
woven strands of hope and trust,
each choice, each heartbeat,
a promise etched in time,
a truth that forever resonates.

So onward you stride,
with fire igniting your heart;
for love calls you to action...
this is where all journeys start.

Eden

Layers upon layers,
known dimensions entwined
with unknown horizons...
the tangible and ethereal,
light mingling with darkness.

Infinite frequencies hum,
the sound of silence whispers,
each pulse a heartbeat of existence.
You and I,
the seed of creation,
the genesis of realities.

Our love flourishes
in the Eden of immortality,
where every heartbeat resonates
with the timeless dance
of dreams woven into life's fabric.

Here, we uncover

the boundless depths of our souls,
echoing in the vast expanse,
as we cultivate our paradise...
eternal and unyielding,
within this sacred sanctuary.

In this hallowed space,
we tend to the garden of our hearts,
each moment a bloom,
each memory a petal,
infusing our paradise
with the fragrance of love.

In The Garden of The Gods

In the garden of the Gods,
I search for you,
where divinity blooms,
and Aphrodite's nectar
fills a golden chalice.

In this sacred space,
a siren's serenade echoes,
swaying to a dance;
the fragrance of jasmine drifts,
mingling with the ballads
of my longing heart.

Here, I shall wait forever for you...
yes, I shall wait
for your eternal embrace,
where love transcends time,
and our souls entwine
like ancient vines in bloom,
woven into the fabric of fate.

In the garden of the Gods,
the air shimmers with promise,
each petal whispering
sweet secrets of devotion,
a testament to our bond
that defies the sands of time,
a love that breathes beneath the stars,
infinite as the night sky.

Eternal soul mates, Past lives whisper forbidden, Love lost in this life.

Vestiges of The Gods

She climbed Wadi's cliffs,
bare feet tracing sacred ground,
ancient whispers rise.

Pangea's remnants,
when oceans cloaked desert peaks...
mountains hold their watch.

Drawn by soul's longing,
in search of tokens and truth,
beyond mortal sight.

Two white shells await,
older than Moses, beyond floods,
keepers of lost time.

She claims them at last,
echoes of ancient love rise,
divine bond restored.

. . .

Layers of Infinity

Peel me a layer
of parallel universes...
bare witness
to a soul's journey,
a cycle repeating,
endless winding turns...

Peel me a layer,
thin veils of onion skin,
and feel tears flow...
my heart beating
a thousand years
of longing...

Peel me a layer
through multi dimensions,
a kaleidoscope mirage:
love caught in a bottle,
trapped in time,
awaiting
the magic of you...

A King's Loot

Crown heavy with gems,
chains of glory hold him still...
lost love fades in gold.

Eyes blind to her light,
seeking truth in empty things,
her throne waits, silent.

He remembers her...
heart bound by forgotten vows,
yet chained to false pride.

When will he let go?
Her love, his royal freedom...
truth's light calls him home.

Immortal Beloved

True love forsaken,
a kingdom's trade for power...
the Jinn's price I paid.

I chose Kingship's path,
the Great Pharaoh's throne of stone;
she, heart of Sumer.

Lifetimes come and go,
twenty and six thousand years,
eternity's toll.

The price was too high,
ancient heart turning to dust,
a thorned crown I wear.

Reborn together,
beneath Babylon's high walls,
a love still forbidden.

Glorious relics,
Oracle of lost empires,
this final cycle.

I shall be with you,
ancient soul, my true flame's light...
soon, you will feel me.

See Me

I traversed through the infinite cosmos,
a Merkaba divine, my celestial chariot.
I danced and danced,
swirled through the Milky Way,
pulled the infinite stardust,
the 8-pointed star.
Light codes dressed me,
I pierced the fabric of time,
pushed through these dense fields.
Yes, I traveled
and took a billion stars
to be here,
to be with you...

I stand before you
on Gaia's glorious, hallowed ground,
a miracle... a stardust... the very cosmos...
I arrived,
unmasked,
with the heavens in my eyes.

But you do not see the universe.
You do not see the stars.
You do not see the cosmos.

I stand before you,
only to find your eyes are shut.
You do not see me.

And I wait for you to awaken.
I shall wait
until the heavens will come to claim
what is borrowed.

I Am here...
See me.

About the Author

ChaCha Israel is a writer, poet, Reiki Shinpiden, quantum hypnosis practitioner, photographer, a successful corporate executive, and an avid traveler whose work explores the depths of divine love, transformation, self-empowerment, and the human spirit's capacity to rise from life's darkest moments.

As a survivor of trauma, single parenthood, and a life-threatening cancer diagnosis, ChaCha discovered that true healing lies in embracing every facet of her story. She has transformed her life through sacred spiritual practices, including Reiki, quantum hypnosis, and Ayahuasca plant medicine ceremonies.

In addition to her book of poetry, ChaCha is the author of the epic saga, Pharaoh Hatshepsut: Daughter of Ma'at, a powerful historical fiction inspired by the first female Pharaoh of Egypt. And Soul

Alchemy: Awakening the Divine Within, a raw and powerful memoir that invites readers on a transformative journey of resilience, self-discovery, and spiritual awakening. Her writing invites readers to embark on their own journeys of healing and self-discovery.

ChaCha's passion is to inspire others to awaken their inner light and embrace their divine potential. She lives in Texas with her beloved husband, Tim, and her children, Preston and Kayla, finding joy in the simple, sacred moments of life. Through her photography and travels, she captures the beauty of the world and the profound connections that transcend borders and cultures.

Ethereal: Whispers of The Soul is a testament to her unwavering belief that within each of us lies the power to transform and transcend.